RALLY CAR RACING
TEARING IT UP

BY BRIAN HOWELL

Lerner Publications Company • Minneapolis

Lerner Publications Company

A division of Lerner Publishing Group, Inc.

241 First Avenue North

Minneapolis, MN 55401 U.S.A.

For updated reading levels and more information, look up this title at www.lernerbooks.com.

Content Consultant: Charlene Bower, Bower Motorsports Media

Library of Congress Cataloging-in-Publication Data

Howell, Brian, 1974–
    Rally car racing : tearing it up / by Brian Howell.
        pages   cm. — (Dirt and destruction sports zone)
    Includes index.
    ISBN 978-1-4677-2121-9 (lib. bdg. : alk. paper)
    ISBN 978-1-4677-2453-1 (eBook)
    1. Rally cars—Juvenile literature. 2. Automobile rallies—Juvenile literature. I. Title.
    TL236.4.H68 2014
    796.7'3—dc23

                                                    2013025293

Manufactured in the United States of America
1—VI—12/31/13

Main body text set in Folio Std Light 11/17. Typeface provided by Adobe Systems.

The images in this book are used with the permission of: © Art Konovalov/Shutterstock Images, pp. 4–5 ; © PRNewsFoto/Subaru of America, Inc./AP Images, pp. 6–7, 12–13, 23, 27; © Maxim Petrichuk/Shutterstock Images, p. 7 (top); © Philip Lange/Shutterstock Images, p. 8; © Hulton Archive/Getty Images, p. 9; © Branger/ Roger Viollet/Getty Images, p. 10; © AP Images, p. 11; © Rodrigo Garrido/Shutterstock Images, p. 12 (top); © PRFrancois Flamond/DPPI/Icon SMI, p. 14; © Francois Baudin/DPPI/Icon SMI, pp. 15, 21 (top); © Karim Sahib/ AFP/Getty Images, pp. 16–17; © Harry How/Getty Images, p. 17 (top); © Marques/Shutterstock Images, p. 18; © Simon Maina/AFP/Getty Images, p. 19; © Mattia Terrando/Shutterstock Images, pp. 20–21; © Greg Kieca/ Shutterstock Images, p. 21 (bottom); © Robert F. Bukaty/AP Images, p. 22; © Roni Rekomaa/AFP/Getty Images, p. 24; © Mikael Hjerpe/Shutterstock Images, p. 25; © Beelde Photography/Shutterstock Images, p. 26; © Andre Lavadhino/Panoramic/Icon SMI, p. 28; © Frederic Le Floc'h/DPPI/Icon SMI, p. 29

Front cover: © Todea Andi/Dreamstime.com (main); © Janis Smits/Shutterstock.com (background).

TABLE OF CONTENTS

CHAPTER ONE

HISTORY AND BASICS

D avid Higgins gripped the steering wheel of his Subaru WRX STI. He looked ahead at a dirt road in the forest outside Portland, Oregon. He was about to start Stage 9. This was one of the 17 small races that made up the 2013 Oregon Trail Rally. The Oregon Trail Rally takes place each year. It is one of the biggest rally car races in the United States. Higgins and his codriver had won the event the past two years. And they had won three of the first eight stages in 2013.

An official counted down from 10. Then he signaled the start of the race. Higgins slammed on the gas pedal. The race began.

CODRIVERS

In many forms of auto racing, a single person drives each vehicle. In rally car racing there is a codriver. The codriver has the very important role of helping the driver navigate. The codriver makes notes about the course ahead of time. These notes help the driver prepare for road hazards or difficult turns. During the race, the codriver sits in the passenger seat. This person gives the driver instructions. This helps the driver keep the car out of danger and complete the course as fast as possible.

Rally car racing is one of the most popular and exciting motorsports in the world.

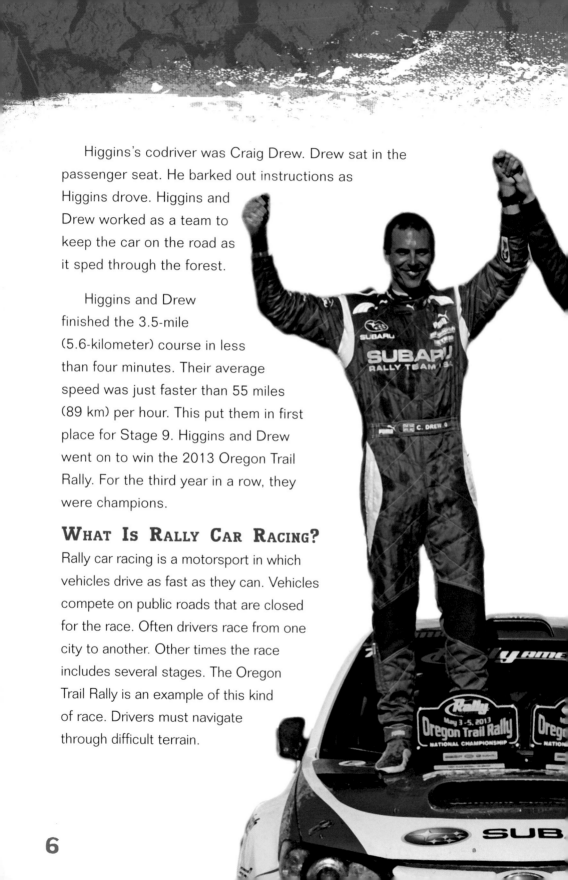

Higgins's codriver was Craig Drew. Drew sat in the passenger seat. He barked out instructions as Higgins drove. Higgins and Drew worked as a team to keep the car on the road as it sped through the forest.

Higgins and Drew finished the 3.5-mile (5.6-kilometer) course in less than four minutes. Their average speed was just faster than 55 miles (89 km) per hour. This put them in first place for Stage 9. Higgins and Drew went on to win the 2013 Oregon Trail Rally. For the third year in a row, they were champions.

WHAT IS RALLY CAR RACING?

Rally car racing is a motorsport in which vehicles drive as fast as they can. Vehicles compete on public roads that are closed for the race. Often drivers race from one city to another. Other times the race includes several stages. The Oregon Trail Rally is an example of this kind of race. Drivers must navigate through difficult terrain.

Rally car drivers navigate many different types of road surfaces at top speeds.

Sometimes the roads are unpredictable. They may be gravel, dirt, or asphalt. They may be wet, covered in snow, or have potholes.

Unlike many other kinds of car racing, rally car racers don't race against one another at the same time. One by one, each car speeds through a course. The driver with the fastest overall time wins the race. Rally car races can be very long. Some races can last for days.

Rally car racing drivers compete because they love the sport. Most rally car races don't offer much prize money. Drivers compete for trophies and bragging rights.

From left: Craig Drew and David Higgins celebrate after winning the 2013 Oregon Trail Rally.

Rally racing cars, such as this Ford Fiesta, are modified versions of regular cars.

Most rally cars are stock cars. Stock cars are like the regular cars people buy at car dealerships. Rally cars often have minor changes from normal cars. They may have better tires or a special roof to make them safer for racing. Drivers can use rally cars on regular streets as well.

EARLY AUTO RACES

Rally car racing first started in the early 1900s. But the sport's roots go back even further. Auto racing can be traced to France in the late 1800s. In 1894 drivers raced 78 miles (126 km) from Paris to Rouen, France. Racers were judged on their driving skills and safety behind the wheel. They were also ranked by speed. In 1895 drivers raced 732 miles

(1,178 km) from Paris to Bordeaux, France. This race was judged on speed alone. Auto racing became more common in Europe in the late 1890s and the early 1900s. At the same time, the sport was becoming popular in the United States.

The first official US auto race took place in 1895. Drivers raced 54 miles (87 km) from Chicago to Evanston, Illinois, and back. One of the first cross-country races in the United States took place in 1905. Drivers covered approximately 4,000 miles (6,437 km) from New York City to Portland, Oregon. The race lasted 44 days.

An event in 1907 was one of the longest rally races in history. Racers drove from Beijing (then known as Peking), China, to Paris. This was a distance of more than 9,000 miles (14,500 km).

Auto racing was a very dangerous sport in its early days. Roads were often unpaved. Vehicles didn't have modern safety features, such as seat belts and air bags. Accidents were common. But drivers and fans still loved the sport.

The Beijing to Paris race was a major event in the early history of rally racing.

In 1912 competitors line up to begin the second Monte Carlo Rally.

THE FIRST RALLY CAR RACE

The Monte Carlo Rally of January 1911 is thought of as the first rally car race. Twenty-three cars competed for first place. They started from various places in Europe, including Paris; Vienna, Austria; and Berlin, Germany. The cars raced to Monaco, a region in western Europe. The starting points were different distances from Monaco, so the cars started the race on different days. Racers drove an average speed of 6 miles (10 km) per hour. They arrived in Monaco on January 28. Frenchman Henri Rougier was named the winner. He drove 634 miles (1,020 km) from Paris.

Other rally car races began to form throughout Europe in the years to come. By the 1950s, the sport had spread as far as Africa, South America, and Canada.

Car manufacturers used early rally car races to promote their vehicles. Rolls-Royce, Mercedes, and other auto manufacturers often entered races. It was a way to advertise their cars. For example, when a Rolls-Royce won a race, that victory would help sell those cars. Some people wanted to drive cars like the ones winning rally races.

MONTE CARLO RALLY

The Monte Carlo Rally is the oldest rally still running. It has taken place nearly every year since 1911. The event has changed over the years. In 1911 cars drove from different parts of Europe to meet in Monaco. Since 1991 the entire event has taken place in southeastern France and Monaco. The finish line is at the Monte Carlo Resort in Monaco.

Rally car races gave car manufacturers a chance to demonstrate what their vehicles, such as this Saab, could do.

THE WORLD RALLY CHAMPIONSHIP

In 1973 the World Rally Championship (WRC) began. This series combined some of the rally events already taking place across Europe. The WRC is still one of the biggest European competitions in the sport of rally car racing.

The WRC has 13 events. Drivers earn points at each event. At the end of the season, the points are tallied. The driver with the most points is named the World Rally Champion. There is also a championship for vehicle companies.

US RALLY CAR RACING

Rally America is a US rally car racing organization. It is based in Williston, Vermont. Rally America is one of the biggest rally organizations in the United States. Rally America was founded in 2002. In 2005 Rally America began its own championship series. The event drew top drivers from around the world.

Rally America holds seven championship events a year. The Oregon Trail Rally is one of these events. Drivers earn points at each Rally America championship race. For example, the drivers with the fastest time in a rally score 20 points. The drivers with the second-fastest time earn 15 points, and so on. Drivers who finish in 10th place or lower score one point.

At the end of each season, the points are tallied. Like most rally racing events, Rally America does not offer prize money. The driver with the most points wins a trophy and the National Championship title. This is a huge honor for rally racers.

Rally America holds some of the top rally car racing competitions in the United States.

CHAPTER TWO

THE RACES

R ally car racing has two main types of events: stage rallies and road rallies. Stage rallies make up many of the events in the WRC and Rally America series. These events sometimes have 20 or more stages. The stages may range in distance from just a few miles to dozens of miles. Road rallies are more like the rallies from the early 1900s. They are long endurance races. Drivers race from one place to another. They drive hundreds or even thousands of miles over days and weeks.

Finnish driver Jari-Matti Latvala races at a 2009 WRC stage rally in Italy.

COLINS CREST ARENA

EDOX

Some rally car races, such as this 2011 event in Sweden, take place on ice and snow, making the course extra difficult for drivers.

STAGE RALLIES

In stage rallies, drivers aim to race through each stage as fast as they can. At the end of the final stage, the total time for each stage is added up. The driver with the fastest overall time is the winner.

Stage rallies are fun to watch. Each stage has a new set of challenges. No stage is quite like the other. Different stages in the same rally may take place on any type of road. This may include city streets to snow-packed mountain roads.

LEADING THE WAY

The Federation Internationale de l'Automobile (FIA) oversees many auto-racing events in Europe. The FIA formed in 1904. It governs some of the world's top rally organizations, such as the WRC. The FIA has main offices in Paris. It has more than 200 members from nearly 125 countries. The United States has two member organizations.

RALLYCROSS

RallyCross is a type of rally racing that takes place on a closed course. Sometimes the course is dirt and marked by cones. Other courses are tracks in stadiums. Some RallyCross courses are city streets. Cars take turns driving through the course. The car with the fastest time wins. In 2006 the X Games added RallyCross racing to its summer lineup. The X Games are put on by sports network ESPN. The X Games holds some of the biggest action sports competitions in the world. It features events such as skateboarding and BMX racing. X Games winners earn medals and prize money. Adding RallyCross to the X Games brought new attention to RallyCross and rally car racing.

One of Rally America's most challenging events is the Sno*Drift Rally. It is held in Montmorency County, Michigan, each January. The Sno*Drift Rally is the only winter event of the Rally America series. It has 20 stages. The stages are driven on ice and snow.

Road Rallies

Since 1993 the FIA World Cup for Cross Country Rallies have been the biggest road rally events in the world. The FIA has eight races each year. The events are held in many places around the world.

One of those events is the Abu Dhabi Desert Challenge. This is a five-day race. It takes drivers more than 1,234 miles (1,986 km) through the Middle Eastern desert.

Rally drivers take part in some of the most challenging events in all of sports. Sometimes they race through short, grueling stages. Other times they drive 1,000 miles (1,600 km) or more.

Brian Deegan competes in RallyCross at the 2011 X Games in Los Angeles, California.

The Abu Dhabi Desert Challenge tests drivers with sand dunes and desert terrain.

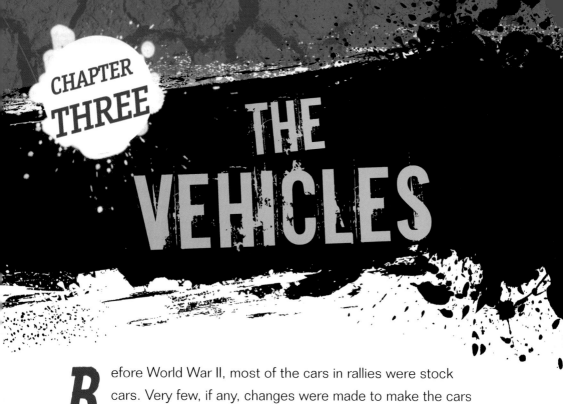

THE VEHICLES

Before World War II, most of the cars in rallies were stock cars. Very few, if any, changes were made to make the cars race better.

Over time the vehicles evolved. Drivers still use stock cars. But many cars are changed to make them more suitable for rally car racing. Drivers use many vehicle models. More than 20 auto companies have cars in stage rallies and road rallies around the world.

Rally cars have modifications that allow them to go as quickly as possible over different types of road surfaces.

Kenyan driver Baldev Chager and codriver Farak Yusuf tear through rural Kenya during the 2007 Safari Rally.

Many rally car racing vehicles are the same makes and models as cars seen on the highway. Audi Quattros, Ford Escorts, Porsche 911 Carreras, and Subaru Imprezas are common cars in rally races. They often don't look like the cars seen on the highways, though. These cars have been equipped for racing.

WILD RIDE

One of the most unique rally races in the world is the Safari Rally. It is held in Kenya, Africa. The Safari Rally was first held in 1953. For many years, the rally was part of the WRC. After 2002 the WRC no longer hosted the race. The Safari Rally still takes place every other year. It is part of the African Rally Championship. Drivers often meet with huge dust storms during the race. They may also see wild animals, such as elephants and lions.

BREAKDOWN OF A RALLY CAR

WINDOWS
Rally car windows are often made of shatterproof plastic. This prevents the driver and the codriver from being cut with broken glass in a crash.

ENGINE
Rally car engines often have a turbocharger. This device makes the engine more powerful. The engines are also built with heavy-duty parts. This makes them less likely to break down during a race.

GRAPHICS
Most rally cars have graphics on them. They include the car's number. They also include the logo of the team's sponsors.

ROLL CAGE

Many rally cars have steel roll cages built into their frames. The cages help ensure the safety of the driver and the codriver if a car flips.

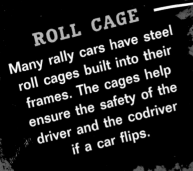

LARGER FUEL TANK

Many rally cars have larger fuel tanks than stock cars. The tank may be made of rubber. This makes it less likely to split or crack in a crash. If fuel leaks during a crash, it could start a fire.

SEATS

Rally cars often have special seats for the driver and the codriver. These seats are extra sturdy. They have harnesses to keep the team safe in a crash.

TIRES

Most rally cars have special tires. Rally tires often have more traction than normal tires. This allows them to handle the tight turns of a rally course without skidding off the road.

BRAKES

Many top-end rally cars have state-of-the-art braking systems. Rally car brakes are often larger than stock brakes. The larger brakes create more friction. This allows the car to stop more quickly if needed.

RALLY SAFETY

Rally car racing can be very dangerous. Drivers race at top speeds around tight turns and on rugged roads. Crashes and rollovers are common. Rally teams take special care to stay safe. Drivers and codrivers wear helmets and fireproof suits. Cars must have fire extinguishers and special seat belts. Officials check this equipment before each race. They make sure it is working properly before the team hits the road.

Rally cars are split into groups called classes. Rallying organizations break down the classes differently. Rally America has seven main classes of cars. The classes are broken into two main categories: Production and Open.

PRODUCTION CARS

Production vehicles must be very close to stock cars. This category is designed for newer rally drivers. Most Production class cars are two-wheel drive. This means only the back two wheels are powered by the engine. Production class cars can only be changed to improve safety or reliability.

Travis Hanson drove a Production GT class car at the Maine Forest Rally in 2006.

Travis Pastrana drove an Open-class Subaru Impreza WRX STI in a 2006 X Games rally car race in Los Angeles, California.

Most Production GT class cars are four-wheel drive. The engine powers all four wheels. Production GT engines often have turbochargers.

The Super Production class allows the most changes in the Production category. Most Super Production class cars are four-wheel drive. They also are turbocharged.

OPEN CARS

The four Open classes allow many more changes than the Production classes. Although the cars have many changes, they must still look like stock cars on the outside.

There are two Open classes for two-wheel-drive vehicles. The cars in one class cannot have turbochargers. The other class is allowed bigger and faster engines.

The Open Light and Open classes are for four-wheel-drive cars. The Open class can make the most changes. These cars have the biggest and fastest engines.

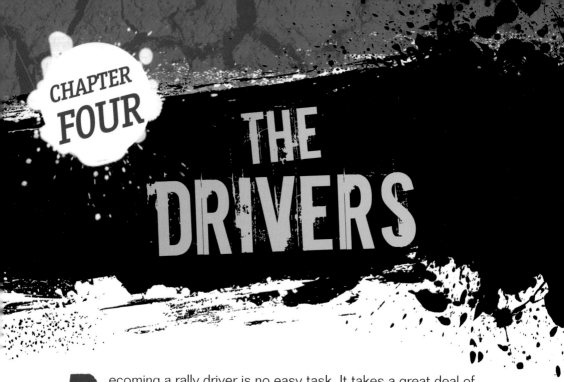

THE DRIVERS

Becoming a rally driver is no easy task. It takes a great deal of practice to fly down the winding roads of a rally course. Many rally car racers get their starts in special training programs. Others join rally clubs. Rally car racing schools are safe environments for new drivers to learn the skills they need to know.

Crews help make repairs to rally cars during competitions.

SPONSORS

Rally car racing can be a very costly sport. It costs even more for drivers who compete in the Open classes. It takes a great deal of money to modify a car to compete in an Open-class rally race. Rally cars are

Driver Ken Block is sponsored by Monster Energy Drink.

often damaged during races. They need to be repaired often. Repairs cost even more money. To help pay for the costs of racing, many professional rally drivers have companies that sponsor them.

A sponsor helps pay drivers who compete in rally car races. Sponsors may also provide parts and vehicles for their drivers. In return, the drivers advertise for their sponsors. The cars and the gear the drivers use may feature their sponsors' logos. Companies that sponsor rally drivers often have close ties to the sport. They may produce tires or other car parts. Many drivers are sponsored by the companies that produce the cars they drive. For example, Subaru sponsors David Higgins. Sponsorships allow some rally drivers to make racing their full-time job.

A TEAM EFFORT

All rally teams need a crew of people to help them out. The crew keeps the car in top shape. Crew members spend countless hours preparing the car for the start of the race. After each stage, the crew goes to work again. It fixes anything wrong with the car. Without the crew, the drivers wouldn't make it through many rally races.

Although Travis Pastrana has retired from stage rally racing, he still competes in RallyCross events.

TRAVIS PASTRANA

US driver Travis Pastrana is one of the best-known extreme sports athletes of all time. He began rally car racing in 2003. In 2006 Pastrana became the Rally America champion. He won the overall championship title for the next three years. Pastrana drove a Subaru in the Open class. For many years, Christian Edstrom was Pastrana's codriver.

On December 31, 2009, Pastrana set the world record for the longest jump ever in a rally car. Taking off from the Pine Avenue Pier in Long Beach, California, Pastrana traveled 269 feet (82 meters) in the air. He landed on a barge floating in the harbor. In 2010 Pastrana left rally car racing to become a NASCAR driver.

DAVID HIGGINS

England's David Higgins won his first rally championship in 1994. Since then, he has won rally races around the world. Higgins won the British Rally Championship in 1997, 1999, and 2002. He drove a Hyundai Accent in those races. In 2002 he came to the United States. He drives a Subaru in the Open class. Craig Drew is his codriver. Higgins won back-to-back Rally America championships in 2011 and 2012. Higgins runs a rally car racing school called Forest Experience Rally School. It is located on 900 acres (364 hectares) of forest in the village of Carno, Wales.

Higgins (right) and Drew (left) celebrate their first Rally America National Championship title in 2011.

SÉBASTIEN LOEB

Sébastien Loeb is one of the most successful drivers in the history of rally car racing. The French driver won nine WRC titles in a row from 2004 to 2012. Before Loeb, the most successful drivers had only won four titles in their careers.

Daniel Elena was Loeb's codriver for all nine championship seasons. Elena is thought to be one of the best codrivers in WRC history. He has always driven a car built by the French auto company Citroën.

At the end of the 2012 season, Loeb said he would no longer drive full-time in the WRC. That put an end to the greatest run of success the sport has ever seen.

DAKAR RALLY

The Dakar Rally is one of the most famous rally car racing events in the world. The first race was held in December 1978. The course went from Paris to Dakar, Senegal. The distance was more than 7,000 miles (11,000 km). Fear of terrorist attacks in North Africa moved the event to South America in 2009. There the event covers more than 5,000 miles (8,000 km). As many as 745 racers from 53 countries participated in the event in 2013.

JUTTA KLEINSCHMIDT

German driver Jutta Kleinschmidt is known for driving long distances. Many people think she is the best female rally racer in the world. Kleinschmidt has been racing for more than 20 years.

Kleinschmidt got her start racing BMW motorcycles in 1985. She began competing in rallies in 1987. In 2001 Kleinschmidt became the first woman to win the Dakar Rally. This event ended in Dakar, Senegal, in North Africa. She drove a Mitsubishi and competed in the T2 class. This is one of Dakar Rally's Production vehicle classes. Kleinschmidt also helped Volkswagen develop a race car called the Race Touareg.

Rally car racing has seen many changes since its beginnings in the 1890s. Each year new courses are developed. These courses challenge some of the best drivers and codrivers on Earth. Rally car racing has become one of the most exciting forms of racing in the world.

German driver Jutta Kleinschmidt has taken on some of the most challenging rallies on Earth.

GLOSSARY

ASPHALT

a tar-like substance often used to pave roads

ENDURANCE

the ability to last a long time

FRICTION

the rubbing of one object against another

GRUELING

exhausting, tiring, or difficult

HAZARD

an object that can cause danger or difficulty

MANUFACTURER

a company that makes and produces cars

NAVIGATE

to direct or help move a vehicle through its course

POTHOLE

a hole in a road's surface

STAGE

one of many parts in a rally car race

FOR MORE INFORMATION

FURTHER READING

Doeden, Matt. *Stock Cars*. Minneapolis: Lerner Publications Company, 2007.

Sandler, Michael. *Rally Car Dudes*. New York: Bearport, 2010.

Savage, Jeff. *Travis Pastrana*. Minneapolis: Lerner Publications Company, 2006.

WEBSITES

David Higgins
http://www.subaru.com/enthusiasts/rally/drivers/david-higgins/index
.html
Visit the Subaru Rally Team USA website to learn about championship-winning
driver David Higgins.

Rally America
http://www.Rally-America.com
Learn more about the drivers, the codrivers, and the races of the top rally series
in the United States.

WRC: FIA World Rally Championship
http://www.WRC.com
The official website of the World Rally Championship features videos, results,
and news about the top rally car racers around the world.

INDEX

ABOUT THE AUTHOR

Brian Howell is a freelance writer based in Denver, Colorado. He has been a sports journalist for nearly 20 years, writing about high school, college, and professional athletics. He has also written books about sports and history. A native of Colorado, Howell lives with his wife and four children in his home state.